# NOTE TO PARENTS

Apologetics Press is a non-profit organization dedicated to the defense of New Testament Christianity. For over 35 years, we have provided faith-building materials for adults. We also have produced numerous materials for young people of all ages.

The Apologetics Press Early Reader Series is a set of books aimed at children in kindergarten through second grade. Depending on the age of your children, this series is flexible enough to allow parents to read to their children, read along with their children, or they can listen while their children read aloud to them.

The books in this series are filled with beautiful full-color pictures and wonderful information about God, His creation, and His Word. These books are written on a level that early readers will enjoy, while drawing them closer to their Creator.

We hope you enjoy using the Apologetics Press Early Reader Series to encourage your children to read, while at the same time helping them learn about God and His creation.

See also our Learn to Read Series for 3-6 year olds and our Advanced Reader Series for 2nd-3rd graders
**www.ApologeticsPress.org**
**(800) 234-8558**

*God Made Reptiles*

by Eric Lyons

Layout and Design by Tommy Hatfield



ISBN-13: 978-1-60063-100-9

Library of Congress: 2014941526

Printed in China

# God Made Reptiles

by
Eric Lyons

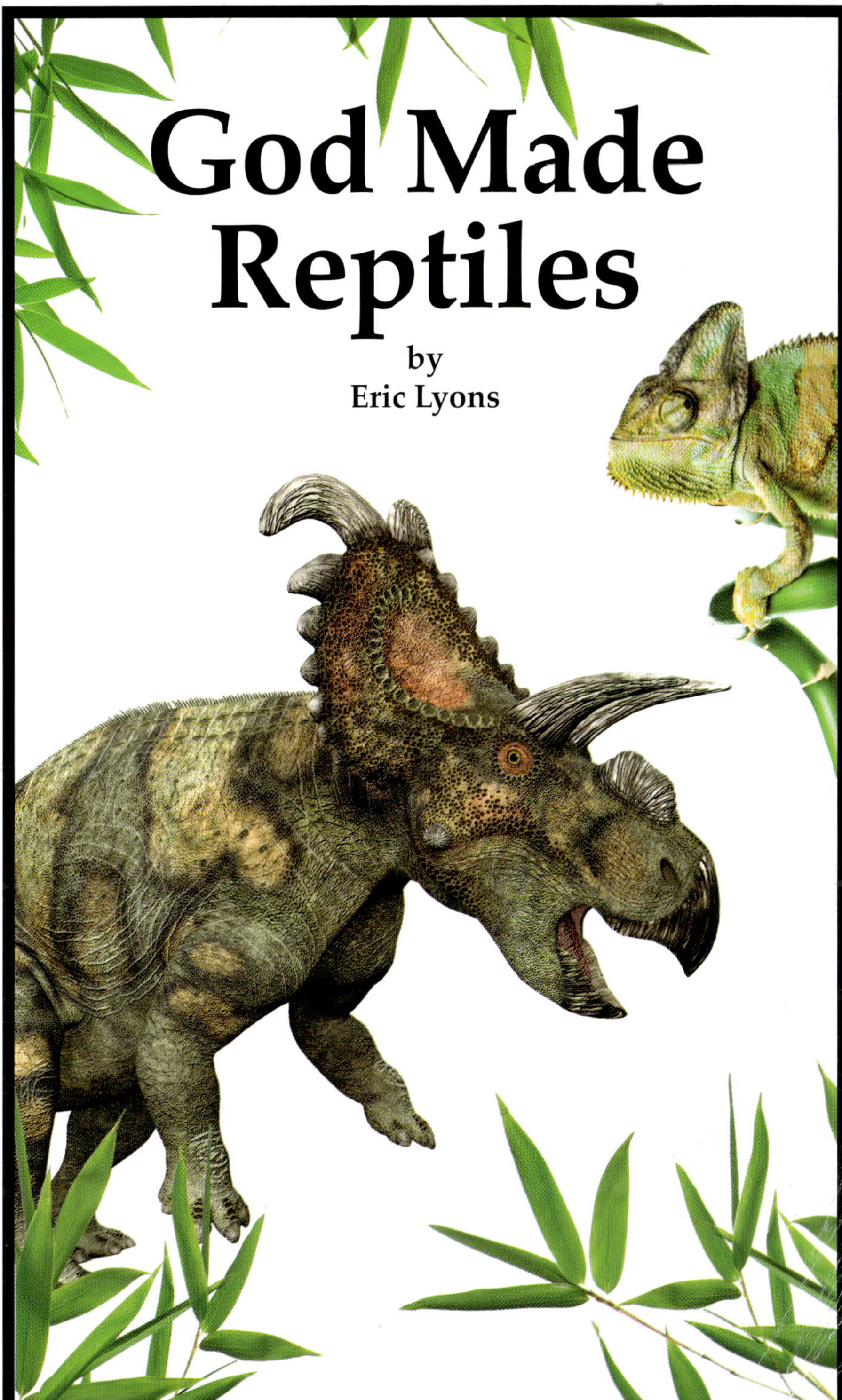

God made many different kinds of reptiles on days five and six of Creation.

He made some
quite small.

While others,
He made very large.

On day five, He created water-living reptiles such as sea snakes and sea turtles.

He also made flying reptiles, such as *Pteranodon* (ter-AN-uh-don) and *Pterodactyl* (ter-uh-DAC-tul). Flying reptiles are now extinct.

On day six of Creation, God made "everything that creeps on the earth" (Genesis 1:25).

He created such reptiles as cobras, chameleons, and komodo dragons.

Unlike mammals such as cows and horses, reptiles are cold-blooded animals.

This means their body
warmth changes as the outside
temperature changes.

Reptiles depend on the Sun and warm places to raise their body temperature.

They normally have dry, tough skin and lay eggs with tough shells.

Snakes are amazing. They can bend, curl, twist, and turn in all sorts of ways.

They can climb up trees, in trees, and down trees. They can slither under-ground or above-ground. They can go across hard rock or loose sand.

God designed snakes with forked tongues. Forked tongues allow reptiles to know where a smell is coming from.

The King Cobra produces venom that it releases through its fangs. Snakes use their venom to kill their prey.

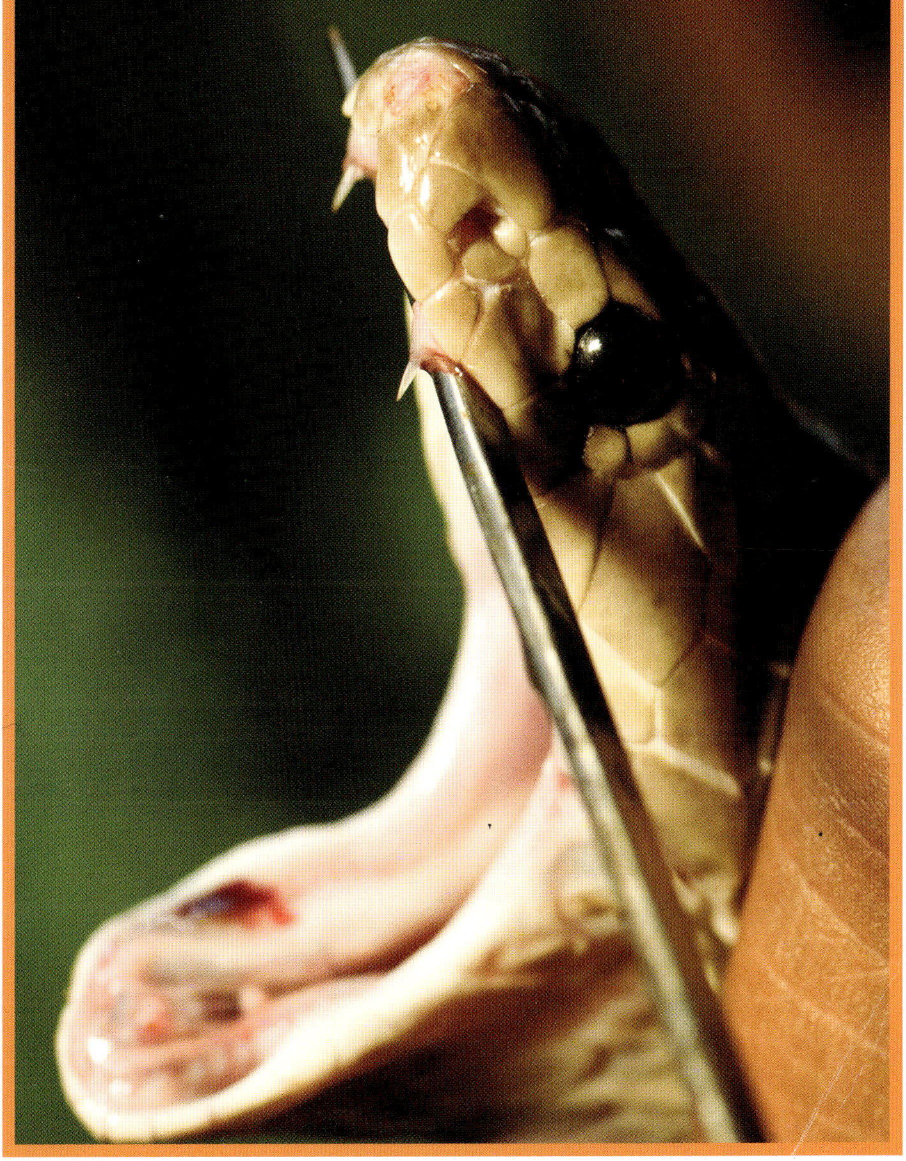

God also designed snakes with jaws that open very wide. Why do you think this is helpful?

Some snakes also live in water. Anacondas, which are the largest snakes in the world, are very good swimmers.

Komodo dragons are some of the heaviest living lizards in the world. They can reach 10 feet in length and weigh over 250 pounds.

Komodo dragons are big eaters. A 100-pound Komodo can eat 80 pounds of meat in only a few minutes.

The Komodo dragon is big, but it is no match for the mighty crocodile. The crocodile can grow over 20 feet long and weigh over 4,000 pounds.

Geckos are loaded with design. They are like little super-heroes that can walk up walls, as well as upside down across ceilings.

The most famous reptiles are those that no longer live on Earth.

We call them dinosaurs.
The word dinosaur means
"fearfully great reptile."

Some dinosaurs were huge—
bigger than a bus.

Most dinosaurs, however, were
only the size of a large cow.

In the Bible book of Job, God spoke about a mighty, dinosaur-like, water-living reptile called leviathan.

It had super-strong scales, "terrible teeth," and "fire" that came out of its mouth.

Other extinct reptiles include the dinosaur-like, flying reptiles.

*Pteranodon* (ter-AN-uh-don) had a body the size of a turkey, but its wingspan was 23 feet across.

Like all other well-designed animals on Earth, reptiles (past and present) are powerful proof of an amazing Designer—God.